Faith Unleashed

Faith Unleashed

How Unquenchable Faith Can Ignite an Unstoppable Life

Clarence Langston

ISBN- 978-1-944662-43-1

Publishing date: January 2020

Affirmation Press

Cover design by Justin J. Dunn, Increase Branding & Design

Dedication

This book is dedicated to my Heavenly Father Jehovah God—I want to thank you for sacrificing your Son that I might have eternal life. I want to thank my Lord and Savior Jesus Christ for being that sacrifice. And I want to thank the person of the Holy Spirit who empowers me with wisdom and knowledge so I can live this abundant life on earth.

To my wife, Robyn Langston, I want to thank you for all of the dedication and sacrifices you have made to God, to me as your husband, and to our wonderful children Gabrielle, Jonathan, and Joshua.

Thank You.

Love,

Clarence

Table of Contents

Introduction

I am so excited you are holding this important life-changing book in your hands! It doesn't matter if you've been a Christian for a short time, a long time, if you're just starting your journey, or if you don't quite believe yet—maybe you have questions about faith and God and how it all fits together in the grand scheme of life. Whatever your spiritual temperature, this book is for you! You're going to learn about the never ending love of God, probe into God's infallible Word, and ask questions that will take you deeper in your faith walk. And in the midst of exploring, your faith will be activated in a mighty way as you embark on a journey that will release in you a deep belief in what God is able to do and WILL do in your life. I feel the power of God even now as I write these Words. By the way, I'm going to refer to Hebrews 11:1 several times throughout this book so you can see the magnificent truths embedded in just this one Scripture.

To start our journey, let's ask: what exactly is faith? **Hebrews 11:1** starts with NOW FAITH IS…

"

It is the substance (or assurance, the "title deed") of things hoped for and the evidence of things not seen.

Hebrews 11:1

What the heck does that mean? Paul is really talking about what faith *does*, not so much what faith *is*. Faith undergirds what we hope for. In simple terms, faith is believing. Faith is the foundation upon which all visible action comes from. When you walk into a building, you don't see the foundation, the unseen support upon which the building stands; you only see the building (the evidence).

I'm here to tell you that your faith is the *unseen* support system for your earthly activity (the things which are seen). And make no mistake, belief without certainty gradually retreats instead of going forward in growth. Faith does not work by the rules of science. Faith allows us to believe that the invisible God can accomplish the physically impossible. Faith dwells on a spiritual plane, not a physical or scientific one and one thing is for sure: there will never be any incongruity between godly faith and true science. Let's continue our faith journey by looking at Hebrews 11: 2-3.

For by it the elders obtained a good report.

Hebrews 11:2

The Word *elders* simply means those who lived long ago; it's not referring to a title. When Paul says they obtained a good report, it means that those mighty men and women of God from the Old Testament who lived godly lives received God's approval. They may be unseen to us today but their example lives on and serves to encourage us to live lives of faith. If those before us utilized faith to overcome and conquer suffering, we can be encouraged to live by faith too since God is still on His throne, and His truth stands firm. Being faithful in progressively larger situations, especially when everything is on the line, demonstrates a mature, living, unwavering faith that allows us to please Him.

By faith we understand that the worlds (ages) were prepared by the Word of God, so that what is seen was not made out of things which are visible.

Hebrews 11:3

Faith is seeing with spiritual eyes the fingerprints of God on His creation. The order, the exquisiteness, the vastness of God's fingerprints are the evidence that God made the world. We see the fingerprints therefore we have evidence. We know He is guiding and directing earthly events in a linear fashion, meaning He has a purpose, a climax that will ultimately come to fruition. God is always driving History to bring about His desired result. Faith is knowing and believing that God is manipulating the course of events throughout the world *and* in our individual lives whether we understand the reason for His methods or not. Our "job", which is our privilege, is to fully yield to His operating agenda.

I get so excited by Hebrews 11:1-3 because it shows that God's whole purpose for giving us faith is so that we can trust in Him as sovereign Creator, Ruler, and Prince of Peace. After all, it's why Jesus came—so God could fulfill His purpose of building and establishing His kingdom here on earth. We are part of that kingdom, beloved ones! The Word I am giving you right now is releasing your faith and feeding your soul; broken like a fresh loaf of bread and poured out like refreshing, cool water.

Faith is recognizing what God has promised so we feel a deep, extensive assurance of things we hope for—this is what Hebrews 11:1 is all about. Faith is an element of creation that we all must use daily. You can't sit in a chair without having faith that the chair is going to hold you—most people never examine a chair before they sit in it, they just sit down. You have to have faith when you get in your car to drive—that you will have safe travels and a safe arrival. Most people never consider the fact they are exercising faith as they travel from one destination to another. The examples I've given are things we do by faith every day and don't even realize it.

The faith I am going to talk about is a greater faith. It is a spiritual inheritance that brings with it a spiritual encounter with God because God wants us to believe that as we work for Him, as we trust in Him, and as we do the will of God, all things will work together for our good. That is why **Matthew 6:33** tells us;

> ***But seek first the kingdom of God and His righteousness, and all these things shall be added to you.***
>
> Matthew 6:33

We are commanded to seek first the kingdom of God and His righteousness, but we often fail to believe the second part: *and all these things will be added to us.* God wants you to know that you are *in* the world but you are not *of* the world. Life is all about you trusting God and believing Him to do His will and in doing His will you know that all these other things, including basic necessities like food and shelter, are going to be added to you. Having "all these things" means that through Jesus Christ, we now have access to all we need. When we truly seek and pursue God with the intent of *only* obtaining the free-access pass, we miss the point entirely. By seeking God's kingdom and pursuing His righteousness, we are already given satisfaction, contentment and grace. Everything else is simply an added bonus.

As we head into the first chapter which overflows with Scriptures about faith, I am going to charge you up, motivate you, and inspire you through and by the Word of God both biblically and systematically. When you read the Scriptures for yourself, your faith is going to be activated and elevated, and as a result, you are going to be able to believe God for anything. You are going to be able to believe God for that new home. You are going to be able to believe God for that new car. You are going to be able to believe God for that promotion on your job. You are going to be able to believe God for increase of every kind. You are going to be able to believe God for anything. This is about your faith and your fate. You are going to learn how to activate your faith which in turn will elevate your fate.

I believe there is something very significant for you here, and as I said, the truth of Scripture stands, so whatever your level of faith, this teaching will shift your thoughts, activate your faith, and then elevate your faith! Hold onto your seat, take a deep breath, and let out a holla to God because here we go!

Questions for Reflection & Study

1. How would you describe your level of faith? Be totally honest with yourself. It's okay to admit you still have questions. If you feel your faith is strong, it's okay to admit that too.

2. How do you know that you have faith?

3. At what times in your life or in what circumstances do you find it more difficult to have faith in God?

4. What are you believing God for today?

1

What Does the Bible Have to Say About Faith?

Plenty!

In this chapter we are going to proclaim, speak, and decree the Scriptures. God has said in His Word in Isaiah 55:11:

It will not return to me empty but will accomplish what I desire and achieve the purpose for which I sent it.

Isaiah 55:11

That means no matter where your faith is today, God will release His Word into your life and your faith will be activated. The caveat is that you are going to have to get out and do what you are believing God for when you activate your faith. There has to be action.

Are you ready?

> ***If you show me your faith by just your Words or just by your conversation he says I will show you my faith by my work.***
>
> James 2:18

Works alone do not save us. Works are evidence that our life has been transformed by Christ. Some people talk a good game. We hear them talking "Christians" and we buy into what they're saying. We might even see them doing good works in the community. But without Christ, works is dead, meaning that our works alone don't bring us into right standing with God; they are of no use or benefit. Works are not added to faith but rather genuine faith includes works.

This means that if someone professes to be a believer and there are no works evident in their life, serious doubt must be given as to the genuineness of that person's faith.

“

And since we have the same spirit of faith, according to what is written, ‘I believed and therefore I spoke,’ we also believe and therefore speak.

II Corinthians 4:13

This is what you are doing right now, you are speaking, so please understand the power of the spoken Word. Continue to speak your faith in Christ despite trials and suffering. You are speaking with the expectation that what you have spoken will happen and that's why it's so important to understand how powerful your Words are.

> ***Faith comes by hearing and hearing by the Word.***
>
> Romans 10:17

This Scripture shows why I am going to speak the Word of God into your spirit. I am going to cause the fire of God, the fire of faith, to ignite you to believe God for everything, even the impossible. That is what faith does—faith causes everything to shift in your favor.

> ***But without faith it is impossible to please Him for He who comes to God must believe that He is and that He is a rewarder of those who diligently seek Him.***
>
> Hebrews 11:6

Just as a married couple cannot please each other with out having confidence in each other, or if there is discord and distrust, God cannot be pleased with the person who has no confidence in Him. How can God be friends with someone who doubts the truth of His Word and the promises contained within His Word? We require the confidence of our spouse and our kids and our friends. How can God not require the confidence and faith of those who profess to know Him? If we have no faith that He hears and answers our petitions, we are not motivated to call on Him. What would be the point? And if our only motivation to seek Him is to get a reward, we have missed the point. But when we diligently seek Him, He rewards us with more of Himself, which includes allowing us to live in our inheritance here on earth, not just in heaven.

And though I have the gift of prophecy, and understand all mysteries and all knowledge, and though I have all faith, so that I could remove mountains, but have not love, I am nothing.

I Corinthians 13:2

Love undergirds our movement, our words, and our faith. We can have a houseful of faith but without love it's nothing more than a fragmented pile of splinters. We are deluded if we believe we can operate our faith without love intimately connected to it. Faith without love is a corrupt faith; and that brings us to nothing.

For we walk by faith,
not by sight.

2 Corinthians 5:7

The Word "sight" is not specifically referring to earthly vision. It's referring to celestial vision as we don't have God in our physical view just yet. When we walk by faith we walk with the expectation that those things which are currently unseen will be made manifest. Our faith will be ultimately turned into celestial vision of the magnificent glories of heaven.

Knowing that the testing of your faith produces patience.

James 1:3

If your mind is singularly focused on spiritual interests, and you are steady in living out God's purpose for your life, you will grow wise and patient through afflictions. Your devotion toward God will remain fervent as you rise above the trials and opposition that test your faith. Afflictions test the truth of your faith—do you *really* believe what God has said? Many people, especially men, say they are not very patient but we must remember that patience is a fruit of the Spirit and God wants us to be fruitful!

Martha said to Him, "I know that he will rise again in the resurrection at the last day.

John 11:24

Martha's faith level would not let her see the power of the moment. Although she was fully convinced Lazarus would rise on the day of judgment, she wanted a different outcome that day and thus was disappointed. When Jesus said, "I am the resurrection and the life" she did not fully grasp the meaning of what His Words meant for her that day. In fact, Martha argues with Jesus about rolling away the stone at Lazarus's tomb because she thought the body would stink from being dead for four days.

Most Jewish people of that day thought that the Messiah would simply be another human being with a special connection to God. They did not believe the Messiah would actually be God incarnate. Jesus is lovingly teaching Martha to move from her belief in Him as Messiah to believe in Him as God in the flesh. Jesus lovingly teaches us to roll away the stone from our dead places and believe He can bring the dead things back to life.

Dead marriages. Dead areas of your heart. Dead hopes and dreams. Maybe some things in your life have been dead for a while and maybe they stink but Jesus is the resurrection and the life. Allow Him to call forth that which is dead and make you alive in Christ!

“

But you, O man of God, flee these things and pursue righteousness, godliness, faith, love, patience, gentleness. Fight the good fight of faith, lay hold on eternal life, to which you were also called and have confessed the good confession in the presence of many witnesses.

I Timothy 6:11-12

When Paul is admonishing young Timothy to fight the good fight of faith he's referring to maintaining *the good combat* as one would have in the Grecian games. Just as contenders in the Grecian physical races strove to lay hold of the winner's crown as the crowd cheered them on, Paul is telling Timothy...and us...to fight for that crown in the spiritual sense—in the presence of many witnesses.

But let him ask in faith, with no doubting, for he who doubts is like a wave of the sea driven and tossed by the wind.

James 1:6

Storm-beaten sailors of the day surely knew what this verse meant, although anyone who has been on a deep sea fishing boat or even cruise ship where rough waters and high waves abound can relate to the metaphor of being tossed by the wind. When a person is not entirely convinced that His request will be fulfilled, His feelings will toss him about like a toy boat in a jacuzzi. One moment hope and faith propel him toward God, then His mind becomes filled with uncertainty and doubt, causing His soul to be agitated and as restless as the ocean. The message in this verse provides the exhortation that when you ask for something, fully believe you already have it.

> ***Jesus said to her, "Did I not say to you that if you would believe you would see the glory of God?"***
>
> John 11:40

Notice the gentle reproof Jesus gave to Martha. Make no mistake, He knows our human emotions and frailties. He was no doubt responding to her when she said, "Lord, I believe." As we rely on the power and faithfulness of Christ, we will see the glory of God. He asks us to take hold of the assurances He has already given us in His Word. He asks of us the same as He asked of Martha, "Only believe."

> ***Jesus said to him, "If you can believe, all things are possible to him who believes."***
>
> Mark 9:23

A father had brought His demon-possessed son to the disciples but they were not able to cast it out. Jesus' statement in verse 23 is most likely directed at the crowd as a whole and not just to the father. Just like in Nazareth, their collective lack of faith threatens to prevent the miracle, but Jesus is demonstrating to them that true faith doesn't presume that God will do what we want, but that God can do what He wants when He wants to. The Father is saying, we all have times of fear and doubt, "I believe but help my unbelief."

But seek first the kingdom of God and His righteousness, and all these things shall be added to you.

Matthew 6:33

According to this verse it is important to seek the Kingdom of God first because when you do, whatever you put your hand to do while exercising your faith in God, will prosper beyond your wildest imagination! You are going to receive everything you believe God for **that lines up with the will of God for your life**. This is what this entire book is about—standing on the Scriptures to align yourself with the will of God. I am not teaching any hocus pocus message telling you to turn yourself around three times and wait for something to happen, because you didn't do anything. You must not merely believe; you have to take affirmative steps toward what you are believing for. I am talking about the solid Word of God. I'm talking about what God is saying pertaining to His children—I am activating your faith even now by the spirit and the presence of God.

Therefore we conclude that a man is justified by faith apart from the deeds of the law.

Roman 3:28

A mustard seed is the smallest seed in the seed family. As a matter of fact, it is so small that if you were to put it in the palm of your hand you can barely see it. Jesus said if you have faith that is so small that most people can barely see, even yourself, if you have even that, you will be able to speak to the mountain and move it from here to there and it will move the impossible for you. Again, I'm not talking a literal mountain but the mountain of your problem, your issue, your need.

“

So Jesus said to them, “Because of your unbelief; for assuredly, I say to you, if you have faith as a mustard seed, you will say to this mountain, ‘Move from here to there,’ and it will move; and nothing will be impossible for you.”

Matthew 17:20

Read those last six Words again…and again. Did you catch that? Nothing, no, nothing, will be impossible for you! I am flying high believing and trusting God to move in your life. You are being blessed as I'm dropping the Word of God into your spirit. You are being inspired. You are being encouraged, but more than that, your spirit is being activated to walk by faith.

> ***But Jesus turned around, and when He saw her He said, "Be of good cheer, daughter; your faith has made you well." And the woman was made well from that hour.***
>
> Matthew 9:22

Jesus was talking about the woman with an issue of blood who had touched the hem of His garment, believing she would be healed. The Bible says this woman had suffered with this health issue for twelve years—that's a long time. She had a situation she had to deal with and believe Jesus for. And that might be you. You may have a situation. You may have an issue no one knows about. The Bible says her faith in His ability caused her issue to turn around. Faith is seeing the outcome visually before it happens. In spite of what your situation looks like you are going to walk by faith. That is what this woman did with the issue of blood. She knew if she could only touch the hem of Jesus garment she would be made whole. The Bible says, Jesus told her "Your faith has made you whole." It wasn't just the fact that she touched him because, remember, there were a lot of people who were flocked around Him, no doubt touching His robe, His hands, His hair, and maybe even His face. The Bible says they pressed in around Him.

My faith right now is fired up for you. The Bible says the letter of the Word kills but it is the Spirit behind the Word of God, the Holy Spirit, that brings the Word of God to life. When you read the Word of God with the faith of God through the spirit of God it causes the life of the Word to come out of the letter. I am sharing this content through and by the Holy Spirit, and as a result, it is activating your spirit. That is why you are getting charged up. You may be reading this at home or at work or on vacation but wherever you are you are being activated right now to trust God and your faith is being strengthened through the Word and also by the Spirit. Without God's Spirit, an individual cannot understand God's Word in the fullest sense, for they cannot have a real appreciation of the spiritual implications of Biblical truth. A person may grasp Biblical thoughts, but miss the life-changing purpose behind the thoughts.

Believe in the Lord your God, so shall ye be established; believe His prophets, so shall ye prosper.

II Chronicles 20:20

My brother, my sister, walk by faith! Things are happening for you because you are believing and trusting God.

> ***Thus also faith by itself, if it does not have works, is dead.***
>
> James 2:17

The significance after you proclaim and stand on the Word of faith, you must go out now to do your part. If you are believing God to open up a door, how can you ever know if the door is open if you never move in the direction of the door. We have to get up and activate our faith.

> ***But to him who does not work but believes on Him who justifies the ungodly, His faith is accounted for righteousness***
>
> Romans 4:5

Paul has already demonstrated in the previous chapter that all have sinned and fallen short of the glory of God (Romans 3:23) and now he's showing the difference between making ourselves right with God through faith and not works. If we could work our way to God, then He would owe us righteousness; our right standing would become transactional. Instead, Paul communicates that it's because of Christ's righteousness that we are made right with him. God does not wait for us to become good enough or godly enough or work enough to "earn" our way to heaven. As we put our faith in the righteousness of Christ, God justifies us in spite of our sinfulness.

> ***Knowing that a man is not justified by the works of the law but by faith in Jesus Christ, even we have believed in Christ Jesus, that we might be justified by faith in Christ and not by the works of the law; for by the works of the law no flesh shall be justified.***
>
> Galatians 2:16

So many people go to church today; they love God but they are trying to justify their faith by the working of the law, by the working of traditions. An example of this might be when a person gets baptized because their mother and their mother's mother got baptized in the same church, or perhaps they volunteer out of a sense of duty instead of love, or they take communion because that's what's always been done in their religion and not because they're remembering and honoring the sacrifice of Christ. According to the book of Mark, the traditions of men have made the Word of God of no effect. In other words, people are practicing religious traditions so much that they won't allow the power of God and the power of faith to come in and change them into the image of Christ. When your faith is activated, you will no longer live as a believer who stands by and watches everyone else be blessed. No! When your faith is activated it causes you to become an active participator in your walk with God.

> ***To open their eyes, in order to turn them from darkness to light, and from the power of Satan to God, that they may receive forgiveness of sins and an inheritance among those who are sanctified by faith in Me.'***
>
> Acts 26:18

The Scriptures keep showing us that there is nothing in the Word of God that keeps us connected to God, and nothing that keeps the power of God flowing to us and through us, except by faith. A man or a woman cannot be saved without faith. Yes, you must believe that He is God, He is the Creator, and that He is sitting high. He comes down to fellowship with us and for that very reason you trust Him and this is also why we walk by faith and not by sight. Even though we can't see the God who fellowships with us with our physical eyes, we must believe in Him and His power.

“

That your faith should not be in the wisdom of men but in the power of God.

I Corinthians 2:5

Notice how I am delivering the Word of God to you. I speak a Scripture and then I show you through and by the Word of God what God has for you. This Scripture is saying for us not to rest in human philosophy. We are in charge of life by our faith in Christ and it's His wisdom, the wisdom of the Word, that we rest in.

Knowing that the testing of your faith produces patience.

James 1:3

The Bible says that the righteous will suffer many afflictions. James is telling us that our faith causes us to endure things that many times we would succumb to if we didn't have faith in God. Our faith assures us that He is going to bring us through our tests. Think about this for a moment. How many times in your life have you lost faith that God was going to bring you out? You doubted His sovereignty and you made a move based on how you felt or what you saw—and it was not the best result for you.

Faith will also give you endurance because it causes you to wait on God while you are doing your part, knowing God is going to do His part. In your testing, God gives you steadfastness and He gives you patience, which is one of the fruits of the spirit. This truth is why I get so excited: as you walk by faith there is nothing you cannot achieve. There is nothing you cannot possess.

May I talk candidly with you for a moment? I have seen God bring so many things into my life; abundant blessings through walking by faith. I have seen Him give me a Cadillac, an Escalade SUV, and a Bentley, and I did not have to pay a dime for any of them. I have seen the miracles of God and the blessings of God. I was homeless as a young man, counted out by different family members, both natural and spiritual. I kept believing that God had a high, holy call on my life and it was manifested…by faith.

When God brought Joseph through His severe challenges after His brothers sold him out, Joseph never sold out God. He kept faith when he was in Pharaoh's house serving as a slave. He kept faith and kept serving diligently when he was lied on and put in a prison cell. He kept faith when it seemed like no one remembered him. And even when it looked like God had forgotten him, Joseph kept faith.

That is the kind of faith I am talking about. Keep the faith no matter what happens! I don't know what situation you are in right now. You may be locked up in a physical prison. You may be in a mental or emotional prison. Let your mind free to serve God. Let your spirit free to worship God. Trust God in every situation knowing that any and every circumstance can change at any moment because you believe God (and I believe God with you). Let's continue.

“

That the genuineness of your faith, being much more precious than gold that perishes, though it is tested by fire, may be found to praise, honor, and glory at the revelation of Jesus Christ

I Peter 1:7

Your faith is more precious than gold to God and that's why He tests it through fire; to purify you, to cleanse you, to build you up in the most holy faith.

> ***Therefore we also pray always for you that our God would count you worthy of this calling, and fulfill all the good pleasure of His goodness and the work of faith with power.***
>
> II Thessalonians 1:11

This verse is a meaty dish in itself but I want to draw your attention to the last part, "...and the work of faith with power." When you turn on a light switch, it's not your power that lights up the room, it's the power in the wires; what's not seen. Likewise, it is the power of God and not your own that begins, continues, and perfects the work of faith.

> ***For in it the righteousness of God is revealed from faith to faith; as it is written, "The just shall live by faith."***
>
> Romans 1:17

You are the just my friend! We have all been justified. That is why I am not talking about the letter of the Word. I am talking about the Spirit that brings the Word to life. But it takes faith. As you read and learn God's Word on your own and at church, is it sinking in that you receive the Spirit by the works of faith and not of the law? Because if you are believing based on the law then it reeks of the flesh and causes men to brag. But if your believing is by faith, it is through and by the blood of Jesus Christ our Lord and Savior. You should be super excited right now as you read this. Don't you feel the fire of God coming up off these pages? That is the energy of faith. There is nothing that you cannot do in Christ!

> ***So then faith comes by hearing, and hearing by the Word of God.***
>
> Romans 10:17

> ***This only I want to learn from you: Did you receive the Spirit by the works of the law, or by the hearing of faith?***
>
> Galatians 3:2

> ***For you are all sons of God through faith in Christ Jesus.***
>
> Galatians 3:26

That means it doesn't matter how you feel. It doesn't matter what somebody says to you or about you. If you know in your heart and are fully persuaded that God is your Father then you are a son or daughter by faith.

> ***Having faith and a good conscience, which some having rejected, concerning the faith have suffered shipwreck.***
>
> I Timothy 1:19

See, the reason why God had you purchase this book about faith is so your faith will not shipwreck. There are many people around us who say they believe God but they have left the faith, their lives shipwrecked in the process.

> ***For indeed the gospel was preached to us as well as to them; but the Word which they heard did not profit them, not being mixed with faith in those who heard it.***
>
> Hebrews 4:2

If you do not have the ears of faith or the heart of faith to receive the Scriptures I am sharing, then it won't work for you. Many of you, as you're reading this book, your faith is being charged, your faith is being built up, and now you know and believe that there is nothing you will not be able to accomplish through and by faith. That is why the Bible says:

"

He who has an ear, let him hear what the Spirit says to the churches.

Revelation 2:29

And the prayer of faith will save the sick, and the Lord will raise him up. And if he has committed sins, he will be forgiven.

James 5:15

Look how powerful faith is! Faith forgives sin. Faith causes men and women to be saved. Faith causes people to enter heaven after death. Faith causes the sting of death to be taken away. God is for His people!

Questions for Reflection & Study

1. **Based on the Scriptures you read in this chapter, which three speak in a profound, intimate way to your spirit? Why?**

2. **Why do you think so many believers struggle with truly believing God for what they want?**

3. **What kinds of challenges and tests have you endured yet you've kept faith in God through it all? Why didn't you give up?**

4. **What action can you take to fully align yourself with the will of God as you pray in faith, believing He will bring what you are asking to pass? Remember, faith without works is dead.**

"

Therefore I tell you, whatever you ask for in prayer, believe that you have received it, and it will be yours.

Mark 11:24

2

Walk in Praise, Prayer, and Purpose

PRAISE

makes you stop thinking about what you are going through. Praise brings focus.

PRAYER

is easy if you praise first.

PURPOSE

is what you walk in as you praise, pray, and operate in God's power.

PRAISE

According to the dictionary the definition of praise means **a**) to express admiration or approval for; **b**) to express thanks and worship to God.

Praise and worship go hand in hand. What it is not is a ritual or "have-to" or a bunch of repetitious Words gushing out of our mouths like Niagara Falls. It's not simply spending five minutes a day reading the Bible or reciting your wish list. True praise according to Praise-and-Worship.com[1] is "a total commitment of our body, mind and spirit. It's about exalting, adoring and acknowledging the God of the Bible. It has nothing to do with religion, but it has everything to do with having an intimate and profound relationship with God - the Father, Son and Holy Spirit." If you worship God, then you love God so much that you don't question him at all. That's praising in faith! God created you to praise Him. He said in Luke 19:40 that if the people didn't praise Him, the very stones would cry out. There is power in praise.

1 Praise-and-worship.com, Praise and Worship the God of the Bible, http://www.praise-and-worship.com/ (accessed on 5/18/2020)

“

But He answered and said to them, “I tell you that if these should keep silent, the stones would immediately cry out.”

Luke 19:40

The key is to praise and worship God for who He is and for who we are IN Him as well as praise Him for who He has placed in our life.

An article on smallgroups.com[2] talks about "worship walks." The article explains how groups of people meet up together in their cars, and then drive to a different location in the city. The group gets out of the car and worship walks around places like schools, courthouses, churches, the downtown areas, health clubs, and I would add, sports arenas, if possible. The article's author describes what it is, "Worship walking is about seeing God at work and praising Him for it. It is putting feet to our prayers as we go to different places in our city." The author encourages participants to read Psalms 100:1-5 and 1 Chronicles 16:8-13, 23-36 out loud on the way to their location.

2 Rudkin, Tami, Worship Walk, SmallGroups.com, https://www.smallgroups.com/meeting-builder/worship-ideas/worship-walk.html (accessed on 9/18/2019)

"

1 Make a joyful shout to the Lord, all you lands! 2 Serve the Lord with gladness; Come before His presence with singing. 3 Know that the Lord, He is God; It is He who has made us, and not we ourselves; We are His people and the sheep of His pasture. 4 Enter into His gates with thanksgiving, And into His courts with praise. Be thankful to Him, and bless His name. 5 For the Lord is good; His mercy is everlasting, And His truth endures to all generations.

Psalms 100:1-5

"

8 Oh, give thanks to the Lord! Call upon His name; Make known His deeds among the peoples! 9 Sing to Him, sing psalms to Him; Talk of all His wondrous works! 10 Glory in His holy name; Let the hearts of those rejoice who seek the Lord! 11 Seek the Lord and His strength; Seek His face evermore! 12 Remember His marvelous works which He has done, His wonders, and the judgments of His mouth, 13 O seed of Israel His servant, You children of Jacob, His chosen ones!

1 Chronicles 16:8-13

23 Sing to the Lord, all the earth; Proclaim the good news of His salvation from day to day. 24 Declare His glory among the nations, His wonders among all peoples. 25 For the Lord is great and greatly to be praised; He is also to be feared above all gods. 26 For all the gods of the peoples are idols, But the Lord made the heavens. 27 Honor and majesty are before Him; Strength and gladness are in His place. 28 Give to the Lord, O families of the peoples, Give to the Lord glory and strength. 29 Give to the Lord the glory due His name; Bring an offering, and come before Him. Oh, worship the Lord in the beauty of holiness! 30 Tremble before Him, all the earth. The world also is firmly established, It shall not be moved. 31 Let the heavens rejoice, and let the earth be glad; And let them say among the nations, "The Lord reigns." 32 Let the sea roar, and all its fullness; Let the field rejoice, and all that is in it. 33 Then the trees of the woods shall rejoice before the Lord, For He is coming to judge the earth. 34 Oh, give thanks to the Lord, for He is good! For His mercy endures forever. 35 And say, "Save us, O God of our salvation; Gather us together, and deliver us from the Gentiles, To give thanks to Your holy name, To triumph in Your praise." 36 Blessed be the Lord God of Israel From everlasting to everlasting! And all the people said, "Amen!" and praised the Lord.

1 Chronicles 16:23-36

She tells the groups, "Pray short simple prayers of praise and thanksgiving for the people who work or live in these places." The author gives examples of the simple prayers of praise the groups can offer up: Thank God for the beauty of this park and for the healthy play that takes place here.

Thank God for the men and women who give their time here to teach our children.

Thank God for the gift of living in a country that allows us the freedom to worship.

The groups typically spend an hour out in the city, worship walking. They will often break out in a song of worship during their praise and prayer time. They all meet back together at a specified time to share what happened and to praise God for any strongholds the group feels were broken during their worship walk. This might be something you can do at your church that could make an incredibly powerful impact on your city.

PRAYER

Some people think prayer is some mystical connection with our "Source" as many personal development gurus advertise. They think you have to touch your fingers together and chant, "ooouumm." Not so! Prayer is intimate fellowship with God. Prayer is worship that glorifies God and reminds us of our need for Him. It's possible to live a life of prayer, meaning we live in an "attitude of prayer." We are simply responding to Jesus's work of salvation and communicating with the very One who created us. So, what's the purpose of prayer? First, we are commanded to pray in the Scripture.

Then Jesus told his disciples a parable to show them that they should always pray and not give up

Luke 18:1

[16]Rejoice always, [17]pray continually, [18]give thanks in all circumstances; for this is God's will for you in Christ Jesus.

1 Thessalonians 5:16-18

[6] Do not be anxious about anything, but in every situation, by prayer and petition, with thanksgiving, present your requests to God. [7] And the peace of God, which transcends all understanding, will guard your hearts and your minds in Christ Jesus.

Philippians 4:6-7

[18] And pray in the Spirit on all occasions with all kinds of prayers and requests. With this in mind, be alert and always keep on praying for all the Lord's people. [19] Pray also for me, that whenever I speak, words may be given me so that I will fearlessly make known the mystery of the gospel

Ephesians 6:18-19

Second, prayer helps us discern God's will for our lives and also helps us make major decisions according to His will.

[12] One of those days Jesus went out to a mountainside to pray, and spent the night praying to God. [13] When morning came, he called his disciples to him and chose twelve of them, whom he also designated apostles:

Luke 6:12-13

Third, and this goes along with praising, prayer gives God the glory for all He is and what He has done in our lives (1 Thessalonians 5:18). Fourth, prayer helps us overcome temptation and struggles.

"Watch and pray so that you will not fall into temptation. The spirit is willing, but the flesh is weak."

Matthew 26:41

If we really, truly realized the power that's available to us when we take our authority in prayer, we would be praying far more than we do. We have all of heaven backing us up! We have authority in Jesus name to witness our lives and the lives of others changed. As believers, we can pray in authority for our neighborhoods and cities, our government and the world. Prayer moves the hand of God! It's a mighty weapon at our disposal as we pray the way God lays out in His Word for us to pray.

PURPOSE

God created you for a divine purpose that He designed before the foundations of the world.

It doesn't matter where or how your mother and father met and conceived you; they could not bring you forth without God. No one is a mistake! No one is an accident! In case you missed it, I'll say it again…no one is a mistake! No one is an accident! God is the life giver and we serve an intentional God. He is the one who allows life to happen so that means God intended for you to be here. He intended for you to be born on the day you were born. He intended for you to survive all that you have lived through. I love to remind people that the Word of God is truth. Think about it: Since He has brought you through everything thus far, I wonder how much more He has for you.

God in His sovereignty has purposed for you to be successful in every endeavor He has called you to walk in throughout your life. It's important to note however that the process to success is not without its challenges. Walking in praise, prayer, and purpose doesn't mean you will not have struggles, challenges, or difficult situations. In fact, God instructs us to praise Him to block out the voice of the enemy. He allows us to commune with Him in prayer so that He can guide, direct, and calm us, and He give us a purpose to pursue. What I love most about God is His preeminence and that He gives us a road map in His Word—the greatest G.P.S. in the world! When we travel to a new place, especially out of town, some of us still use a paper road map although the majority use the navigation system on our phones or in our car. We tap into that navigational system if we want the most efficient route to our destination. Some systems will even tell you if a car is stopped on the side of the road or if there is law enforcement somewhere nearby or it will take you on an alternate route if there is a traffic jam. Well, I'm here to tell you that God's Word is our navigational system. He knows the pitfalls we will face, the potholes we will stumble into, He knows the dangers ahead and He can untangle the traffic jams that gnarl up our minds as we make our way through this world. The good thing to know is that as a believer, when you believe all things are possible, there is nothing you cannot achieve in God according to your faith. There will be hindrances in life, there will be distractions in life, there will be problems and situations that come up, but things that hold you back cannot stop you when your faith is activated.

Many times, we experience internal conflict and that conflict is rooted in our lack of trust. We have faith but we see the tornado spinning all around us and we waver a bit. We may ask, "God, are you sure you know what you're doing in this circumstance?" You have to get to the point where you say, "Father I believe you regardless of what I am going through or how I feel." The enemy wants to take your trust because where there is no trust, there is no faith. Just like in Habakkuk 2:3, we must believe, "Though your vision tarry it shall come to pass."

“

For the vision is yet for an appointed time; But at the end it will speak, and it will not lie. Though it tarries, wait for it; Because it will surely come, It will not tarry.

Habakkuk 2:3

Never get comfortable in what you see. There are different stages or seasons we go through in life, but in every stage we must continue to exercise faith. God is FOR YOU and that is more powerful than the whole world or the devil against you. Stay the course, keep believing.

> ***And let us not be weary in well doing for in due season we shall reap, if we faint not.***
>
> Galatians 6:9

God said He will bless you exceedingly abundantly above all you can ask or think. I am here to activate you to walk in faith. I want you to start saying "Amen God, I am in agreement." I want you to start moving again toward your dream and toward your vision as God is prompting me to tell you that though the vision He gave you may tarry it is coming to pass. God has made a pathway for you and the pathway is based on your agreement with God's divine order.

The number three in the Bible is the number of divine order; completeness: Father, Son and Holy Spirit. Everything God did He did through the power of agreement. The Bible says a threefold cord is not easily broken—you may be able to break a string or a strand but you are not going to be able to break a rope with your hand. Agree with God right now for your vision, your purpose. I remember the power I felt come upon me when I came into agreement with God the

Father, God the Son, and God the Holy Spirit. The three are wrapped up in one; the divine order completeness releases the free gift of God's grace and there is nothing that happens in the earth or in your life without God's grace. Do you now see how important being in agreement with God is in order to fulfill your vision and purpose? Praise the Lord that He loves you in spite of you and since His Word is truth, it will come to pass no matter what is happening around you.

I want to encourage you! You are about to see the promise of God fulfilled in your life according to your ability to trust God more than you trust yourself.

Your issues have not been a God issue, they have been a faith issue!

You have been through many circumstances through the years but now those things are about to work in your favor. It is according to your faith and your ability to believe God. There is a Word that you must get back into your lifestyle and that Word is YES. Say yes to His will. Yes to His way. You may not understand everything going on around you but you have to believe in and say yes to the Word of God. You may be in a dilemma but God is giving you a Word and that Word is, "Trust Me." God is turning it in your favor. And what that means is: things right now that appear not to be working out for you are about to work out for you. And the things that have been coming up against you are going to get behind you and act as a mighty wind to push you forward.

Yes, God is going to propel you into a place where you need to be but you are not there yet. I need you to have enough faith in what you are reading—men and women of God are called to bring you good news, not trouble. Forget about your trouble, the trouble is going to work *for* you, if you trust God. If you continue walking by faith no matter what your situation looks like, no matter what your circumstances seem like, no matter what people say about you, walk by faith. No matter how anything appears, walk by faith.

And always remember this: for every door that closes in your face God will open up doors that will take you further than that one door you depended on. That spouse who didn't value you, God will give you somebody who is going to value you. That financial ruin you thought you'd never recover from; God will bring abundance of every kind into your life. That death of a loved one that crushed your spirit so hard that you thought you'd never feel whole again, God will bring healing, wholeness, and refreshment in ways you never thought possible. So don't worry about the closed doors; just celebrate the open ones! As you walk in praise, prayer, and purpose, God will align your will with His and you will experience breakthroughs like never before.

Walk in praise, prayer, and purpose!

Questions for Reflection & Study

1. **How will you celebrate and praise God for your open doors? Will you shout hallelujah? Sing? Dance? Tell someone else to encourage their spirit?**

2. **What do you think your purpose is for God's kingdom? Have you taken a spiritual gifts test? Do you know what your gifts are?**

3. **Write about a time when God closed a door you thought was perfect for you and then He carved a newer, bigger, wider door for you to step through.**

4. **In what ways are you walking in praise, prayer, and purpose? Are you struggling with one of those areas? If so, which one? What one thing will you do to improve that area?**

“

For we walk by faith, not by sight.

2 Corinthians 5:7

3

Standing on the Promises During Difficult Times

I want to share with you some revelation from Heaven that will reveal some promises and blessings that God has ordained for your life. And I want you to have a spirit of expectation that things are going to start happening in your life as you move closer to what God has promised you. In this chapter, not only will I inspire you, I am going to motivate you to put your faith into action so you can see it at work in your life on a daily basis.

There are so many promises God has set for you. As long as you are in agreement with His will for your life, all His promises are yes and amen. However, you have a role to play—you must be obedient to His Word and know that it is impossible to please Him without faith. When you go to God you must absolutely know that He is, and that He is a rewarder of those who diligently seek Him. For you to know the promises of God for your life, you must read His Word and develop a prayer life. You don't have to be a Bible scholar to read His Word...just read it...the Bible says His Word will not return void, it will accomplish what it sets out to do and God says in Isaiah 55:11.

> ***it shall accomplish what I please,***
> ***and it shall prosper in the***
> ***things for which I sent it.***
>
> Isaiah 55:11

You don't have to pray eloquent, lofty King James prayers. Sometimes, it's just a matter of acknowledging who He is and thanking Him for all your blessings. At other times, it's as quick as "Help God, I need You!" Remember that God is waiting to hear from you; He loves to hear from His children just like you like to hear from your children. It will put your mind at ease knowing that God has you in mind. God is faithful to His Word. Everything and everyone around you may fail you but God will never fail you. The Word of God is powerful and life changing.

God's Word is your heritage. You have to get it "into you" so you can fight off unbelief and every troubling circumstance that seeks to snatch your faith. The troubles of this world will pass away but God's Word will never pass away and that's why it's so crucial that you read it, memorize it, and love it with everything in you. John 1:1 says:

> ***In the beginning was the Word and the Word was with God and the WORD WAS GOD.***
>
> John 1:1

God upholds all things by the Word of His power and that Word will come to pass in your life! Here are a six Scriptures to stand on and build your faith during difficult times. I want you to feed yourself and meditate on the power contained within each promise.

9 The Lord also will be a refuge for the oppressed, A refuge in times of trouble. 10 And those who know Your name will put their trust in You; For You, Lord, have not forsaken those who seek You.

Psalm 9:9-10

The Lord is good to all, And His tender mercies are over all His works.

Psalm 145:9

***Fear not, for I am with you;
Be not dismayed, for I am your God.
I will strengthen you, Yes, I will help you, I will uphold you with
My righteous right hand.***

Isaiah 41:10

These things I have spoken to you,
that in Me you may have peace.
In the world you will have tribulation; but
be of good cheer, I have overcome the world.

John 16:33

[6] ***Do not be anxious about anything, but in every situation, by prayer and petition, with thanksgiving, present your requests to God.*** [7] ***And the peace of God, which transcends all understanding, will guard your hearts and your minds in Christ Jesus.***

Philippians 4:6-7

I can do all things through
Christ who strengthens me.

Philippians 4:13

I don't know what it is you're believing God for today but as you come into agreement with Him and do your part, that thing you're believing Him for is coming to pass in your life even now as God moves on your behalf.

> ***'Not by might nor by power, but by My Spirit', says the Lord of hosts.***
>
> Zechariah 4:6

Please know that it is not by *your* might that the promises of God are going to come to fruition in your life, nor is it by *your* power. When you look at the Word "might" I want you to see man's strength. That thing you want to happen is not going to happen by or through your own strength. It is not going to happen by man's power nor by man's influences; who you know or what you know can only take you so far. Mankind is limited but God is not limited. I don't know about you but I will always make the choice to NOT operate in my own human power especially knowing that my authority outside of God has limitations. But IN GOD there are no restrictions! There are no limits even if things seem to be delayed. You may be thinking, *how is this going to happen because you said there is nothing I cannot do, and there is nothing I cannot achieve*. You may have tried to accomplish something but you tried to get it done in your own power. Zechariah said in verse six, "...But by my spirit saith the Lord of hosts." I want you to see how powerful God is and how God's Spirit moves in the earth. Even though you are limited by your ability, you can have faith in God's ability to do for you what you can't do by or for yourself.

We've read in a previous chapter that **Hebrews 11:1** says:

> ***'Now faith is the substance of things hoped for, the evidence of things not seen.***
>
> Hebrews 11:1

When you look at Hebrews 11:1 and you truly understand what that verse is saying; *now faith is...* Is what? Faith is the *substance of things hoped for*. There has to be an expectation attached to your faith or it's no faith at all. What kind of life are you living if you have no expectation? A life with no expectation is no life at all. It is void of excitement. With no expectation you are not moving toward promise. You are not moving toward gain. You are not moving toward achievement.

God wants you to understand that when you operate in this level of power it is power that comes from above; not by earthly means, nor mental means, nor willpower means, nor any kind of manmade means. The earthly realm is always shifting. You don't know what to expect from one day to another. Witnessing on a daily basis how the earth is continually changing reminds me of how we as human beings are continually changing. We can be so wishy washy in our own power and in our own strength—one day we are up and the next day we are down. In one moment, everything is happening for you and in the next moment it seems like everything has dried up. You are human and you live in a physical body so you know what I am talking about.

Life has a funny way of going. You never know from one phone call to another what to expect when you say hello. Someone who is here today may not be on the earth tomorrow. With that thought in mind, you must understand that you don't have the power you think you have outside of God. It's only IN God and THROUGH God that true and lasting manifestation can happen and isn't it nice to know that you serve a God who has an endearing, unflinching love for you and holds the power for everything you desire according to His will. He loved you enough to send His Holy Spirit as an indwelling power after you accepted Jesus Christ as your Savior. See, when you were born the first time you were born of flesh because Adam sinned and all humankind fell short of the power of God. That means we were once all spiritually lost because of sin but the good news is that Jesus Christ the Redeemer paid the penalty for our sin. When you make Jesus Christ your Lord and Savior, you become born again; born of the spirit. He is our power source! He is where we get our power!

Once you become born again, the Holy Spirit comes to live *in* you and you can then ask God to baptize you with an empowering overflow of the Holy Spirit coming *upon* you. The Holy Spirit is a person. He is not a thing and He is not an emotion nor a feeling. It's like plugging your spirit into a never-ending, always-present power source. Understanding the power of the Father, Son, and Holy Spirit and how they work together takes faith and that's what I'm teaching you.

Anything I do in Jesus name and I stay consistent and keep taking action, even when it looks like what I'm believing for is not coming to pass...keep believing... it is going to happen... yet if I don't do anything, nothing is going to happen.

You cannot let this world's system and life control who you are and how far you go. You cannot allow the family you have been born into determine your fate. Nor can you depend on how far up or how far down your family history has gone to determine your fate. It doesn't even matter how successful you and your immediate family have been, whether in marriage, finance, or business, it doesn't determine how far you will go. You cannot allow anything or anyone to be a hindrance in your life. Please understand, YOU are going to be the one who breaks the mold. If cancer runs in your family, cancer cannot and will not come through you. If your family has not experienced a strong educational heritage, then it begins with you. If your family has experienced drug or alcohol abuse, the generational cycle ends with you. You have power through the Holy Spirit and whatever you believe will come to you and will be attracted to you by your thoughts—embrace and understand who you are in God!

By leading you into a faith walk I am building your faith for what you are about to step into. **1 Corinthians 2:9** says, **Eye has not seen nor ear heard nor have entered into the heart of man the things which God has prepared for those who love Him. Yet often people stop at that verse and never get to verse 10 which says, But God HAS revealed them to us through His Spirit. For the Spirit searches all things, yes, the deep things of God.**

What that means is *the things that God has prepared for you* are already in place. They're yours NOW! He who goes before you is more than the world against you. God is saying to step over into your breakthrough. He is Jehovah Jireh, our Provider! He is Jehovah Nissi, our banner! Jehovah El Roi, the God who sees! He is Alpha and Omega, the beginning and the end—the whole enchilada as they say. In the movie Lion King the characters called the world "the earth" and light the "circle of life" because everything comes full circle. Appointed once a man to be born and appointed once a man to die— the circle of life. God said, "I am Alpha and Omega. He didn't say I am Alpha and in the middle. A complete circle goes all the way back around to the same point that it started. That means that God, Jesus, the Holy Spirit are all encompassing and all eternal.

I am building your faith to know that as you put God first everything else in your life will line up. One thing I have learned about God is that if you take care of His business, your business will line up with His perfect will. When you put God first and trust Him, things that are out of order, or seem out-of-place, including your children, your love life, your relationships, your career will all begin to come together as you have envisioned. Things, events, situations in your life start to align when you put God first. This is the part of taking action I'm talking about: Are you believing God for a husband and you don't fix yourself up at all? Are you believing God for a wife and you don't have a vision for your own life? You have a part to play! Put God first and take action and watch God do it for you.

One of the biggest challenges to praying during hard times is continuing to stand when things look hopeless. It's a true test of faith and perseverance. The story of David and Goliath is a perfect example of how to stay in the fight during difficult time. David as a young boy was able to defeat a big, bad giant with only a slingshot and a rock. David already knew that God would protect him because he has already experienced God's victory over the lions and bears. David was not about to slink back in fear because he had seen God at work in past circumstances. Victory in God makes us strong and bold and builds our faith for the bigger battles. Now, Saul tried to suit up David in His armor but just like a kid who plays dress up in His parent's clothing, the armor didn't fit. It was cumbersome, weighty, clunky. God had already designed a way for David to fight in the way that fit him. Same goes for us! We are each equipped with gifts and talents to wage war on our giants and we have Biblical strategies to help us in the fight. David knew he wouldn't kill the giant in His own strength. He knew it would be through the power of God he would defeat the Philistine and that God would get the glory for the victory.

It's during our most difficult times that we need to rely heavily on the Word of God and what it says about overcoming rough and tough circumstances, difficult people, combating false accusations, our own emotions, and of course, the fiery darts of the mortal enemy himself, Satan. We might wonder where God is when the walls are closing in around us, when our hope is losing ground, when our faith has been shaken to its core, and when we feel broken and lost and confused. I'm here to tell you to lean on God's promises because they were written to encourage us and so we'll come to know God's wonderful character in a deeper, more intimate way. God's promises can override our feelings and refresh our mindsets. We can go from defeated and deflated to experiencing jaw-dropping awe of God's precious promises fulfilled on our behalf.

Questions for Reflection & Study

1. **Describe something you are believing God for. Have you been obedient to what His Word says? What actions are you taking that line up with God's Word when it comes to what you are believing Him for?**

2. **What giant are you facing right now? Are you looking to the power of God to defeat that giant?**

3. Have you asked the Holy Spirit to come upon you, to fill you to overflowing with God's power and might? Tell about your experience, or if you haven't, ask Him right now to baptize you in the Holy Spirit.

4. Say this out loud several times. Write it out and tape it to your bathroom mirror: I cannot be stopped! Everything God has promised me in His Word shall come to pass!

4

Believe God for The Impossible

“

So then faith comes by hearing, and hearing by the word of God.

Romans 10:17

In Romans, the Word tells us that faith comes by hearing and hearing by the Word of God. Thus, as a believer, it is imperative that we speak what is good and right and what edifies us. In fact, our life paths respond to what we hear and what is spoken. For example, have you ever gone to the doctor and they tell you that you have a certain condition and then for days or weeks afterward it seems like that condition gets worse or progresses faster after they say it? The doctor didn't mean any harm; they were just doing what they were supposed to do. But once you heard it you got in the car and all of a sudden it seemed like your body started responding to what you heard. Well, I, too, am delivering you a prognosis, however, I am telling you what God has purposed for your life and what He has called you into. Hallelujah! I am bringing you the good news that there is power in the name of Jesus and that nothing is impossible for God.

In John 16:7 Jesus is talking to His disciples, ***But very truly I tell you, it is for your good that I am going away. Unless I go away, the Advocate will not come to you; but if I go, I will send him to you.***

While He was on the earth, the disciples saw Jesus lay hands on the sick and witnessed each one recover. They saw Him cast devils out of children, men, and women. They saw the lives of men and women instantly changed. They prospered because He spoke into their businesses.

Do you remember when Simon was out fishing as part of His profession? It was common for fishermen to put their nets out in the water all day and then pull in the fish at the end of the day. The Bible says Peter and the other fishermen had put out nets all day and caught nothing. Maybe you can relate on another level. Have you worked all your life and it looks like you don't have anything to show for your effort? That's probably what these fishermen felt like at the end of a long day. Jesus simply told them to cast out their nets again and this time the nets were so full of fish, they started to break. The same power Jesus operated in is given to us by the Holy Spirit. As we speak and decree by faith, things will happen. When Jesus is involved in any endeavor, the result is increase and favor.

Increase is on the horizon—I decree and declare it. I want you to get this: YOU HAVE THE POWER in Jesus' name. Let me explain. During the summer Olympics there are relay races in which runners pass a baton to one another during the race. Whoever gets the baton is responsible for running and the race isn't over until all the runners on the relay team pass the baton and finish the race. In the New Testament, Apostle Paul gave an analogy about running a race.

1 Corinthians 9:24-27 - ***Do you not know that in a race all the runners run, but only one receives the prize? So run that you may obtain it. Every athlete exercises self-control in all things. They do it to receive a perishable wreath, but we an imperishable. So I do not run aimlessly; I do not box as one beating the air. But I discipline my body and keep it under control, lest after preaching to others I myself should be disqualified.***

Paul tells us it's how we finish the race and that we should run to win. In 2 Timothy 4:7 Paul says about himself, I have fought the good fight, I have finished the race, I have kept the faith. Jesus passed this baton to us as believers. He has given us authority to not merely fight but to win. Do you hear me—YOU WIN!

When you are trusting Him and walking by faith, anything can happen. There will be times when you are walking with God that you are going to be embarrassed because you are going to speak out regarding circumstances you are believing Him for and at the time everything will look contrary to what you say. See, some of us are what I call "secret faith agents" because we speak our wants and needs in secret because we don't want to be embarrassed if those things don't happen. That is not faith. You have to put yourself out there. You must walk and proclaim boldly what you are believing for. Some may think you have lost your mind. You have to truly walk in this thing called faith or what you're believing God for is not going to happen. And get this: it's not going to happen just because you think really hard about it. What you are believing God for is not going to happen if your words are not coupled with faith. If there is no faith to go along with your words, your words are meaningless. Faith coupled with action is what will get you where you want to go. And as a result, you will come into everything you desire that lines up with God's will for your life and God will get all of the glory from it.

What kind of impossible things has God done?

The stories are too numerous to tell here but let me just hit on three. First, there is Abraham. Before he even had a child, God gave Abraham a promise that His descendants would be more than could be counted. God compared Abraham's descendants using the imagery of stars and sand to demonstrate the vastness and Abraham believed God before there was any proof. Not only did God fulfill His promise in a natural way, He fulfilled it in a spiritual way as well because all who receive Jesus Christ as their Savior are counted as children of Abraham. Galatians 3:29 - **"And now that you belong to Christ, you are the true children of Abraham. You are His heirs, and God's promise to Abraham belongs to you."**

Second, Abraham's faith was tested again when God told him to sacrifice Isaac as a burnt offering. Isaac was older by then and could have easily overtaken His dad when Abraham was tying him to the altar but he trusted His dad's relationship with God. An angel stopped the sacrifice because Abraham's faith was proven strong.

God is invested in our strength and the only way our strength muscle can grow and develop is through working it out by testing it and stretching it. How strong is your faith muscle today? Those who hold the greatest trust in the Lord are those who have witnessed Him guide them through the fiercest of trials. It's in those fiery trials that God shows Himself faithful and trustworthy.

Third, the impossible happened when God accepted us through Jesus Christ. He met us exactly in the place where we were and brought us into His family. The cool thing is that He doesn't leave us where we are! He cleans us, transforms us, makes us brand new.

What is YOUR impossible situation? Do any of the following resonate with you?

- Having a baby when doctors say you're unable to
- Leaving your current job to start your own company
- Paying off your mound of debt
- Becoming financially independent
- Meeting and marrying the spouse of your dreams
- Healing from disease or physical ailment

God says nothing, no nothing, is impossible with Him! The caveat in that statement is to remember that it's God's Word that will be fulfilled, not our own. If we're honest, sometimes we may hear things that we believe are from God but they're really not so we must test what we hear against God's Word and counsel to confirm if they are or aren't what God is really telling us.

Are you ready to believe God for the impossible today?

If so, find your anchor Scripture. Claim your promises. Write the vision. Pray in faith and then thank Him ahead of time for it. Your Father delights to do the impossible but our beliefs must be in line with God's will. When we live in obedience to God's will, nothing is impossible! Proclaim right now, "God, I know you can do what I'm believing You for. I know that You are able. But if you don't answer in the way I'm expecting, I will still worship You and honor You because my praise is all about who You are."

Questions for Reflection & Study

1. **What have you been toiling at for a long time and not seeing results?** ***Will you yield to the powerful words of Jesus that speak increase and fruitfulness into your life?***

2. **What kind of "impossible" things has God already demonstrated that show us He can be confidently believed when He speaks?**

3. What will you boldly proclaim to others no matter what the reaction?

4. If we're bound up in the snares of sinful living it will slow us down in the race. Are there any hinderances or weights that you need to cast off so you can run freely and swiftly?

5

You Shall Reap in Due Season

“

Believe on my prophet and so shall you prosper.

II Chronicles 20:20

It is due season and when it is due season it is a new season. How you choose to respond after you read this book will determine if you are entering a new season in your life. After reading and studying about faith, if you go back to your same old thinking, acting like those same old situations have victory over you then you are the same person in the same exact place. Faith causes you to shift direction.

Remember, when praises go up they pierce the darkness that comes to hinder us from seeing daybreak. That darkness is the enemy trying to break down your door with confusion—to try to cause you to believe that the sun could never break through and penetrate these dark places. No matter what you are going through, when you praise God you break out of what the enemy has been trying to hold you in. If the enemy is trying to hold your body or mind hostage to His wiles, begin praising God and don't stop until your body and mind start to act right. If you have family members who have gone astray and you don't see any hope for their redemption, start praising God until they come back into right relationship with God Almighty. If you are experiencing financial oppression and loss, start praising God and see deliverance come to your door. That doesn't mean you sit on the couch and wait; get to work and watch God open the floodgates of provision and abundance in your life. Praising God in faith "the evidence of things not seen" moves His hand in your favor.

The old saints used to sing a hymn that included the words, "Jesus is on the main line so tell Him what you want." Back in the day there was a main line and a party line. Everybody could get through on the party line but not everybody could get through on the main line. **I am trying to tell you how to get your breakthrough and how to get your deliverance. I am trying to tell you how to get your turn-around. I am trying to tell you how to come in to your new season. It is by faith.**

You must believe God is a Healer *before* you believe in your healing. You must believe He is a deliverer before you believe He wants you delivered. You must know that He wants to save you and also know what He wants to save you from. This is a wicked and perverse generation where people are sick and full of demonic spirits—spirits that cause people to hurt and kill other people. As believers when you get a hold of salvation and are delivered from spirits that once tried to rule you then you are delivered from voices that try to make you believe that it is not going to get any better than where you are right now.

No weapon formed against you shall prosper, And every tongue which rises against you in judgment You shall condemn. This is the heritage of the servants of the Lord And their righteousness is from Me," Says the Lord.

Isaiah 54:17

Please know this—the devil is a liar. His mission is to steal, kill, and destroy and he'd like nothing more than to destroy your spirit and kill your faith but the good news is that he doesn't have the final say! Our God has the final say! God says, your best days are ahead of you. God says he delights in the prosperity of His people. God says He IS Victory! This is your due season and this is your new day. Some of you have been tormented by demonic spirits. Some of you have been tormented by prescription and non-prescription drugs. Some of you have been tormented by alcoholism. Others have been tormented by cigarettes. Cry out right now to the Lord God Almighty and claim your deliverance because where the spirit of God is there is liberty, there is healing, there is breakthrough. God is a God of power and might! He hears you right where you are! Don't wait to clean yourself up before you come to Him. Right now is the time! By faith receive what God has been waiting to give you.

> ***Behold, I stand at the door and knock. If anyone hears My voice and opens the door, I will come in to him and dine with him, and he with Me.***
>
> Revelation 3:20

Notice…He's knocking. You must answer the door because He won't bust His way in.

Once God transforms your heart, His desire is to make you holy as He is holy. It's been said that God is not so much concerned with your happiness than He is with your holiness. And don't get it twisted; holiness is not a style it is a lifestyle! Every believer is called to be holy and the good thing is, God doesn't leave you to get holy by yourself. He empowers you to be more than a conqueror. God loves you so deeply and so fully, He just can't take His eyes off of you. I get so excited when I talk about these things because I have been where you are today. I have gone through those faith levels and dimensions. And now I am going through new faith levels and dimensions. The older saints used to tell me, "New levels, new devils." What they didn't tell me is what happens spiritually at each new level. As you deal with your different faith levels the enemy will try to steal your peace, your family, and your purpose.

The thief comes but to steal to kill and to destroy but Jesus says I am the good Shepherd; I come that you might have life and that you might have it the more abundantly.

John 10:10

I don't know about you but that sounds like increase to me. I do know that as you praise God, you will increase.

James 2:14 says faith can never manifest unless there is work with it. So if you believe God to do something in your life then there are things you must do. Changes you must make. Don't depend on anything visible to make you whole. If God blesses you with a car, thank God for that car, but know that it is just a car and it doesn't make you whole. Anything outside of yourself can't make you whole. Because God is in you and around you, you don't have to reach outside of yourself to receive God. Once you receive Him by faith your spirit which was once lying dormant because of Adam's sin comes back to life. Through Adam's sin, sin came into the world. Through another man's obedience, *Jesus, the 2nd Adam*, salvation came in. You were once dead to God and alive to sin but once you accepted God's free gift of salvation you are now dead to sin and alive to Jesus.

There is nothing outside of you that can make you greater than what He created and purposed for you to be. So you should not seek a house to make you whole. You can desire a new house but it won't make you whole. You desire it because you want a new house but you can't depend on it to be the answer to your deliverance because you already have a Deliverer. The name of your deliverer is not Rolls Royce, it is not Tesla or Lamborghini, it is not designer clothing or name brand five thousand dollar shoes, nor is it the latest gigantic movie screen for your home theatre. Your Deliverer's name is Jesus! He and He only is the answer to problems. The Bible says at the name of Jesus every knee shall bow and every tongue shall confess that He is Lord. Diabetes, you have to bow at the name of Jesus. Cancer, you have to bow at the name of Jesus. Divorce, you have to bow at the name of Jesus. Attached to the name of Jesus is grace which means God gives you His unmerited favor; favor we don't deserve but because

He loves us He still gives it to us. If you notice, there are five letters in the Word g-r-a-c-e and that is what number five represents: grace, and grace transcends failure of any kind.

You might have failed yourself. Your parents may have failed you. Your teachers may have failed you. But God will never fail you! I'm teaching you how to really trust God and know that it is your season. To everything there is a season and **now** is your due season.

What to do in your season…

Habakkuk 2:2 says write your vision down. A vision is a plan. God gives you a plan for your life and then it is up to you to write it down and to nurse it, rehearse it, and work it. Remember the Word of God concerning your life. The Bible says God is ahead of you and if God is ahead of you then He has already made a way for you where there was no way. But, you have to keep moving forward. Don't stop, get it get it.

If the storms of life are trying to take away your faith in God's ability and your ability to complete the task in front of you, whatever you do, don't stop…keep moving. It is due season for your breakthrough and break out. What does that mean? It means keep moving forward until you get everything God has promised you according to your faith in His ability to do more for you than you can do for yourself. Let no person, no downfall, no opposition stop you from coming into all God has already done for you. You need to know you are victorious. What does it mean to be victorious? It means you are a winner. Walk and talk like the winner you are!

Questions for Reflection & Study

1. What new season do you believe God is bringing you into?

2. In what ways is the enemy and His oppression trying to rob and kill your dream, your desire, your destiny?

3. What do you know about God now through reading this chapter that you can use to combat the enemy and His tactics?

4. What is your vision? Write it down. In what ways will you nurse and rehearse your vision?

5. What does walking victoriously mean to you?

6

God's Got You

Do you know that your steps are being ordered by God?

> ***The steps of a good man are ordered by the Lord: and he delights in His way.***
>
> Psalms 37:23 23

What exactly does it mean that God is ordering your steps? Does it mean it absolves you of all initiative and action? No way! It is good and right to plan. Just like you read in the previous chapter, write your vision down. However, you need to recognize that your plans will only succeed if they are in line with God's will for your life. **James 4:13–15** - *Come now, you who say, "Today or tomorrow we will go to such and such a city, spend a year there, buy and sell, and make a profit"; whereas you do not know what will happen tomorrow. For what is your life? It is even a vapor that appears for a little time and then vanishes away. Instead you ought to say, '**If the Lord wills**, we shall live and do this or that'.*

“

In your heart you may plan
your course, but the
Lord determines your steps.

Proverbs 16:9

Sometimes we align our plans with God's purposes. At other times God overrules our plans. Truthfully, sometimes we get it wrong and thankfully it is the Lord who determines our steps and will turn us back around to His path. Occasionally, it's human opposition that seeks to derail what God has planned for us. Paul certainly experienced this in **Acts 22** although he knew that God would ultimately and strategically order His steps. The sovereignty of God means we don't have to worry about our ultimate outcome. God is in complete control, even though it may not always be easy for us to see it. God's got you! We as believers are always victorious. This I know, for the Bible tells me so.

God often works out His purposes through good leadership. Good leaders motivate others—they do not base their decisions simply on what is popular: *Sound leadership has a moral foundation* (**Proverbs 16:12b, MSG**). They cultivate an environment of transparency, *Good leaders cultivate honest speech; they love advisors who tell them the truth* (**Proverbs 16:13, MSG**). *They invigorate lives; they're like spring rain and sunshine* (**Proverbs 16:15, MSG**). Do you see now? It's not just waiting for God's direct voice that our steps are ordered. He uses His foot soldiers and our action to accomplish what He wills for us.

Thank you, Lord, that although I make plans in my heart, ultimately you determine my steps. In making my plans, I always say, "If it is the Lord's will…" **Psalms 143:8**—*Show me the way that I should go.* You have to consistently believe that the promise of God is going to happen for you. If you are going through a setback or disappointment, remember **Romans 12:2**.

> ***His purposes for you are good, pleasing and perfect.***
>
> Romans 12:2

Nothing happens without God's permission.

Romans 8:28 shows us that God is in control and *in everything* he is working for your good.

> ***And we know that all things work together for good to those who love God, to those who are the called according to His purpose.***
>
> Romans 8:28

Mark the Word of God concerning your life. Many times we are not prepared for the storms that come our way—they sneak up on us. Just like a natural storm—you can be outside and you can hear thunder but the sky looks clear and you're looking around like *where is that thunder coming from*. Well, it was so high above the sunshine you didn't even realize a thunderstorm was looming. There are storms in front of many of you today but I want you to be encouraged because the storm that is coming is going to help you, it is going to fortify you, and it is going to equip you for where you are going. All through the Bible we read about men and women who went through storms by God's divine plan but ultimately came out more powerful and stronger than before. One example is Peter after he denied Jesus. He went out at the time and wept bitterly yet he was a cornerstone of the new church of believers in Acts. Jesus saw Peter's heart and wasn't going to let him go too far out of His reach. In Peter's epistles, this big burly fisherman uses the Word precious seven times. Peter states that Jesus is precious because He shed His blood for us. He also says that the Lord Jesus is precious because of the faith and grace and Word we received from Him.

God gave His only son, which means you are precious to Him. I will let you in on a little secret: it has always been about you when it comes to our Heavenly Father. The world tries to make us believe that He is light years away from us, that He is some heavenly body way up in the sky, distant and foreboding. That is not the case at all. As believers, we have the Holy Spirit living inside our hearts at all times. That's why **Psalm 46:1** says He's an ever-present help in time of need. God has blessings in store for you that your physical eyes have not seen. *In store* means they are stored up just for you to grab hold of as you walk in His steps.

Let us therefore come boldly to the throne of grace, that we may obtain mercy and find grace to help in time of need.

Hebrews 4:16

Faith is believing without proof or evidence so those who are about to be blessed are those who still believe God's promises although they don't see one stitch of proof. Faith is a Word used to describe believing, and believing is used to describe faith, because they are not the same. You can believe but if you don't put action, which is your faith, to what you believe it won't come to pass. Without faith we don't please Him and when we don't please Him we don't get what we are asking for; plain and simple. It's time to work your faith.

Questions for Reflection & Study

1. **How have you seen God ordering your steps in life?** *When were you in the right place at the right time and something great happened? Or, have you been five minutes late to leave for somewhere and later find out you avoided a bad accident or harmful incident?*

2. **When have you found yourself going the wrong way and God did a course correction to bring you back into alignment with His steps?**

3. In what ways have you witnessed God using His foot soldiers *and* your action to accomplish His will in your life?

4. Write down 2-3 Scriptures from this chapter that were particularly meaningful to you that pertain to what you are believing God for. Memorize at least one this week.

7

Faith and the Incomprehensible Love of Christ

I Corinthians 13:4-8 - *Love suffers long and is kind; love does not envy; love does not parade itself, is not puffed up; does not behave rudely, does not seek its own, is not provoked, thinks no evil; does not rejoice in iniquity, but rejoices in the truth; bears all things, believes all things, hopes all things, endures all things. Love never fails. But whether there are prophecies, they will fail; whether there are tongues, they will cease; whether there is knowledge, it will vanish away.*

Love sounds perfect, doesn't it? Jesus's love IS perfect! He demonstrated His love through actions according to who He was; He was true to His character. That is why you need to understand that love is not an action as much as it is a person. If you are a certain kind of person, your actions will reflect who you are. Many people claim they have God in their lives but the question is: does He *have* them? Paul wrote letters to the church of Corinth but those same Words are for us today, that you would know that even though you may not feel it sometimes, God still loves you with an incorruptible, incomprehensible, indescribable love. Since Jesus paid the penalty for sin there is no sin hanging onto you once you receive Him as your Savior. Now, don't get it twisted, you still have a sinful nature and that is why the enemy works so hard to get you to believe that you don't *have* to receive Jesus as your Savior.

The enemy deceives you into believing that as long as you are a good person, that's good enough. No! Believers in Christ will only know you by the manifestation of the fruit you produce. Apple trees don't bear peaches. Peach trees don't bear apples. They bear fruit based on the type of tree they are. Some of you reading this might feel offended when you go to your job and you tell people you are saved and they say, "Nah, you are not saved." And you say, "Yes I am saved!" They are simply saying that because they don't see your life or language or behavior bearing godly fruit. The fruit of your life will most certainly manifest and that is why they don't believe you are saved. If you're swearing, listening to water cooler gossip, listening in on the latest dirty joke, and being slothful at work, your fruit speaks for itself. But thanks be to God in that He still loves you in spite of you although as a believer your life needs to bear fruit from being connected to the Vinedresser, Jesus. The fact is we all make mistakes each and every day and He still loves us so much.

Faith is connected to love and love is connected to faith. You might say they're interwoven. Your salvation is connected to faith. You cannot walk daily in God's true love without walking in faith. When you bring faith and love together in your daily life you will begin to bear much fruit and you will know without a doubt that nothing is impossible as you abide in the Vine and walk according to His will. God is love and to say you love God means that you'll look for ways to put your love into action and that is where your faith comes into play. It is Christ living inside of us that gives us loving hearts for our fellow believers and those in the world. The incomprehensible love of Christ dwelling in our hearts manifests itself as we, in turn, love those around us. How are you showing God's incomprehensible love to your spouse today? Your kids? Your close and extended family? Your friends? Your church body? Your co-workers? The homeless person? Employees of the places you do business with? Yourself? **1 John 3:14** says, "We know that we have passed out of death into life, because we love the brothers." Let Christ love on you today! Let Him fill you to overflowing with who He is.

Meditate on the following Love Scriptures

Psalms 143:8 - *Cause me to hear Your lovingkindness in the morning, For in You do I trust; Cause me to know the way in which I should walk, For I lift up my soul to You.*

Proverbs 3:3-4 - *Let not mercy and truth forsake you; Bind them around your neck, write them on the tablet of your heart, and so find favor and high esteem in the sight of God and man.*

I Corinthians 13 - *And now abide faith, hope, love, these three; but the greatest of these is love.*

I Corinthians 2:9 - *But as it is written: "Eye has not seen, nor ear heard, nor have entered into the heart of man the things which God has prepared for those who love Him."*

Proverbs 10:12 - *Hatred stirs up strife, but love covers all sins.*

I John 4:8 - *He who does not love does not know God, for God is love.*

Mark 12:30 - *And you shall love the Lord your God with all your heart, with all your soul, with all your mind, and with all your strength. This is the first commandment.*

Lamentations 3:22 - *Through the Lord's mercies we are not consumed,*

Because His compassions fail not. They are new every morning; great is Your faithfulness.

Questions for Reflection & Study

1. **Do you consider yourself a "good person" but don't see the need for a Savior? If so, go back and re-read this chapter. We are all in need of a Savior no matter how good or how bad we consider ourselves to be.**

2. **How has the incorruptible, incomprehensible, indescribable love of Christ affected your life?**

3. What kind of fruit are you bearing? In your family? At work? With friends?

4. List a few ways that love and faith are working together in your life. Are there any areas you need to shift to align more with God's love?

8

Powerful Testimonies of Faith

As you read these two testimonies, allow both life-changing outcomes to release your own faith that God is willing and able to do for YOU what you are asking Him for.

Testimony 1 – this is a first-hand experience I personally witnessed during a Sunday morning worship service.

As I was ministering the Word of God during a Sunday morning service I spoke out that court cases were being cancelled. A mother grabbed ahold of the Word I spoke because her son was incarcerated. Not only was he incarcerated but he had ten different charges against him with two different judges. She went to Alabama (she lives in Michigan) where he was incarcerated. She spoke to the judge and asked him if her son could come back home. The judge replied, "No, he has to serve His time." The judge continued, "Ma'am, since your son has been here for a few months we will let him go next month." The mother told the judge, "No, because that is not what the prophet said." The mother stood on the Word of the prophet and did not waver. Her son was released. But as she was completing His paperwork something came up on the computer for another crime he committed in another city. With that, the court could not let him go. So, she came back home to Michigan without her son.

The next Sunday service I spoke another Word that court cases are being thrown out. This mother snatched the power of the Word again and did not give up. She traveled back to Alabama to go before another judge on her son's behalf. She had been told beforehand that this particular judge was very tough. She continued to speak the Word that court cases would be cancelled. The judge told her that her son would not be released. She did not waver. Even though she was told no the first time she stood on God's Word that I spoke, not to her directly, but while I was ministering in service. Her faith was released through what God has spoken through me that day. Not only did she believe in what I spoke in God's name but she put action with her faith. So, whatever you are believing God to do it is your faith along with action. This is a truth I have repeated throughout this book, and for good reason—it works!

> ***So then faith comes by hearing, and hearing by the Word of God***
>
> Romans 10:17

Testimony #2 – This next account was widely publicized in 2015 and also prompted the making of the movie, Breakthrough, so you're probably already familiar with it, but all the same, the story shows how faith can make a difference between life and death.

On January 19, 2015 John Smith, fourteen years old, adopted at five months old from Guatemala by Joyce and Brian Smith, fell through the ice at Lake Sainte Louise. He stayed submerged for about fifteen minutes before emergency workers found him and pulled him out of the frigid water. John wasn't breathing and first responders performed CPR on him for almost forty-five minutes but His pulse never returned. They rushed John to the hospital and Dr. Kent Sutterer, the lead ER doctor, held little hope since he had never seen anyone survive after being without a pulse for more than twenty-five minutes and a pH level below survival range. Dr. Sutterer called John's mother, Joyce, into the room to tell her son goodbye since he knew that any further life-saving attempts would be futile. When Joyce entered the room her first reaction was to start praying out loud. She said, "Lord, Holy Spirit, just give me back my son!" Seconds later, John's heart began to beat although His condition was still extremely critical.

Once John was stabilized he was airlifted to Cardinal Glennon Children's Medical Center in St. Louis. Lead pastor of the Smiths' church, Jason Noble, and five other pastors, gathered in John's room to pray. While praying Pastor Noble said he saw a vision of two angels in the room and lights over John's head. According to an article by Susan Weich, reporter for Saint Louis Post-Dispatch, Pastor Noble is quoted as saying "What I believe is that God was putting His brain back together again, almost rewiring it. I know that sounds strange, but as soon as it happened, John's shoulders came off the bed, His eyes opened, and he grabbed my hand. I knew at that point that God was going to pull him through." Fifteen days later John Smith walked out of the hospital.

See what faith does! Believe. Cleave. Receive.

Questions for Reflection & Study

1. **Write down once again what exactly you are believing God for today. Be very specific.**

2. **How does reading the two testimonies of faith release your own faith that you will receive what you are asking of God?**

3. Write down the next action you will take to release your faith.

4. After reading this book, where would you say your faith is on a scale of 1 – 10?

Conclusion: Ignite Your Faith!

You have read the Word of God throughout these pages and no doubt your faith has been stirred. You have been encouraged in your walk with Christ as you've gained a deeper understanding of what it means to walk by faith and also how to activate your faith. You should know without a shadow of a doubt that there is nothing the Father will withhold from those who believe in Him and believe that He is a rewarder of those who diligently seek Him. In your seeking, I encourage you to re-read this book whenever you feel like you need a faith boost.

I hope and pray you've realized that God never fails! I exhort you to never waver in your faith even when it looks like nothing is happening because it *has* already happened in the Spirit and your faith will allow it to manifest in your life.

You have the victory! Walk in your victory. Walk in His power. Walk in His strength. Own it. Live in it. Stand tall and stand strong. The Bible says stand still and see the salvation of the Lord. I pray you will live a life of faith in and through Jesus Christ.

About the Author

Apostle Clarence Langston is the Founder and Senior Pastor of Word In Action Christian Center in Detroit, Michigan. Langston zealously answered the call to salvation at the age of twenty, after experiencing numerous trials and tribulations. During His younger years, he was drawn to street life which ultimately found him fearing for His life. Soon after that, Langston received the call to salvation. He then served in numerous facets of ministry for nearly twenty years. In 2006, Langston founded Word In Action Christian Center, in Detroit, MI. Anointed with a rhema Word from God, he teaches with an unwavering boldness. As an apostolic reformer, he is called to perfect the saints by imparting biblical truths, emphasizing deliverance and spiritual warfare, and activating the gifts of the Spirit in order to develop strong disciples and ministries in the body of Christ. He has a strong apostolic and prophetic call and fathers the sons and daughters of God by equipping and empowering them to live holy, prosperous lives with unshakeable faith.

Langston has been given a "Kingdom Agenda" and will not stop until the vision God has given him comes to pass. Langston has traveled throughout the United States preaching the Gospel of Jesus Christ. He is the host of "The Crossover" which can be seen daily on Impact Network. He is the former co-host of the cable television show "Get Connected" and radio broadcasts on 102.7 FM, WHPR in Detroit and WEXL 1340 AM, on *Morning Glory with Clarence Langston.* He has been featured in numerous Christian and secular magazines and has appeared as a guest on Christian television station TCT's "Celebrate Live Detroit," the Word Network's "Rejoice," and Impact Network's "Impact Today." ClarenceLangston is a man who is in authority as well as under authority. He serves His spiritual parents, Chief Apostle Wayne T. Jackson and Dr. Beverly Y. Jackson, as a board member of Impact Network. Langston has also produced numerous, powerful CD series. He also joined the cast of Oxygen's "Preachers of Detroit" where he proudly shared his love for his family, his faith and his city, with the world. He is joined in ministry by his lovely wife, Pastor Robyn and has three beautiful children.

Also I heard the voice of the Lord, saying, "Whom shall I send and who will go for us?" Then said I, "Here am I: send me."

Isaiah 6:8

How to Order

To secure Clarence Langston to speak at your church service, leadership meeting, conference, or retreat, to order bulk copies, or to request media interviews:

Website: ***www.ClarenceLangston.com***

Phone: 313-864-5300

Email: ***admin@wiacc.com***

C L Ministries

19780 Meyers Road

Detroit, Michigan 48235

If you're a fan of this book please tell others…

- Write about ***Faith Unleashed*** on your blog and social media channels.
- Suggest this book to your friends, family, neighbors, and coworkers.
- Write a positive review on Amazon.com.
- Purchase additional copies for your church team, retreat, or to give away as gifts.
- Feature Clarence Langston on your radio or television broadcast.

CPSIA information can be obtained
at www.ICGtesting.com
Printed in the USA
BVHW041834040920
587805BV00003B/237